PowerKids Readers:

Eating Right

Elizabeth Vogel

The Rosen Publishing Group's
PowerKids Press™
New York

1

Published in 2001 by The Rosen Publishing Group, Inc.
29 East 21st Street, New York, NY 10010

First Edition

Book Design: Felicity Erwin

Layout: Emily Muschinske

Photographs by Thaddeus Harden
Illustration (p. 5) by Emily Muschinske.

Vogel, Elizabeth.
    Eating Right / Elizabeth Vogel.
        p. cm.—(PowerKids readers. Clean and healthy all day long)
    Includes bibliographical references and index.
    Summary: This book describes the five main food groups and how eating right promotes good health.
    ISBN 0-8239-5686-5
    1. Nutrition—Juvenile literature. 2. Health—Juvenile literature. 3. Food—Health aspects—Juvenile literature. [1.Nutrition. 2. Health. 3. Food.] I. Title. II. Series.
    2000
    613.2—dc21

Manufactured in the United States of America

Contents

There are five main
food groups:
1. Bread and cereals
2. Fruits and vegetables
3. Milk and other dairy foods
4. Meat and other protein
5. Fats, oils, and sweets

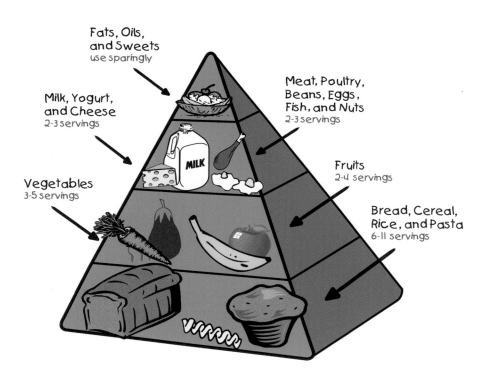

Milk, Yogurt, and Cheese
2-3 servings

Meat, Poultry, Beans, Eggs, Fish, and Nuts
2-3 servings

Vegetables
3-5 servings

Fruits
2-4 servings

MILK

Bread, Cereal, Rice, and Pasta
6-11 servings

The Food Pyramid

I eat breakfast every day.
I need food to start
my day.

7

We like to run around outside. We need energy to do this.

9

I share carrots with my mom. Carrots are vegetables. Carrots have vitamins in them. We need vitamins to stay healthy.

My mom measures how tall I am. It is important to eat foods that are healthy. Healthy foods help your body grow big and strong.

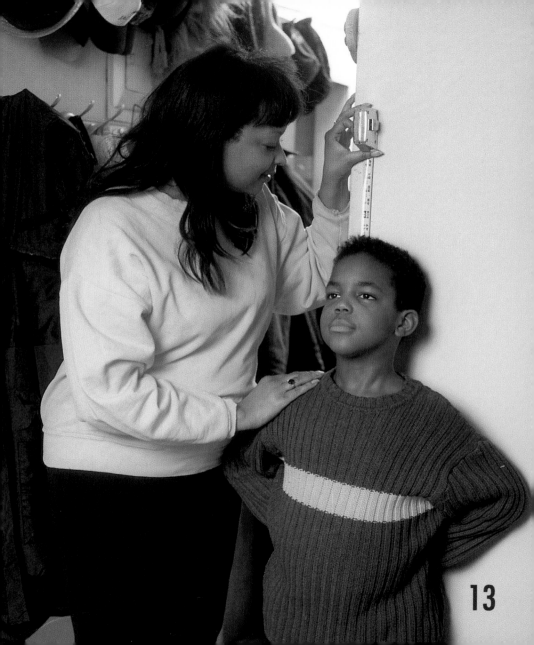

13

I always have a drink with my food. The drink washes the food down. I have juice, milk, or water.

15

Sometimes I have a cookie after a meal. Dessert foods like cookies have lots of sugar. A little sugar tastes good, but too much is not healthy.

An apple is a great snack! Snacks are little bits of food to keep you going between meals. I like snacks.

Try to eat right every day.
Eating right will help you
feel healthy all day long.

21

Words to Know

APPLE

BREAKFAST

COOKIE

DRINK

VEGETABLES

Here are more books to read about eating right:
Nutrition: What's in the Food We Eat
by Dorothy Hinshaw Patent
Holiday House, Inc.

The Food Pyramid
by Joan Kalbacken
Children's Press

*Good Enough to Eat: A Kid's Guide
to Food & Nutrition*
by Lizzy Rockwell
HarperCollins Juvenile Books

To learn more about eating right, check out
these Web sites:
http://exhibits.pacsci.org/nutrition
http://www.freshstarts.com

Index

Word Count: 178

Note to Librarians, Teachers, and Parents

PowerKids Readers are specially designed to get emergent and beginning readers excited about learning to read. Simple stories and concepts are paired with photographs of real kids in real-life situations. Spirited characters and story lines that kids can relate to help readers respond to written language by linking meaning with their own everyday experiences. Sentences are short and simple, employing a basic vocabulary of sight words, as well as new words that describe familiar things and places. Large type, clean design, and photographs corresponding directly to the text all help children to decipher meaning. Features such as a picture glossary and an index help children get the most out of PowerKids Readers. Lists of related books and Web sites encourage kids to explore other sources and to continue the process of learning. With their engaging stories and vivid photo-illustrations, PowerKids Readers inspire children with the interest and confidence to return to these books again and again. It is this rich and rewarding experience of success with language that gives children the opportunity to develop a love of reading and learning that they will carry with them throughout their lives.